MARJORIE HARRIS
FAVORITE
SHADE PLANTS

Photographs by **PADDY WALES**

HarperCollins*PublishersLtd*

First Edition

Canadian Cataloguing in Publication Data

Harris, Marjorie
    Marjorie Harris favorite shade plants

ISBN 0-00-255409-7 (bound)
ISBN 0-00-638040-9 (pbk.)

1. Shade-tolerant plants – Canada. 2. Gardening in the shade – Canada.
I. Title.   II. Title: Favorite shade plants.

SB434.7.H37 1994   635.9'54   C94-930694-0

94 95 96 97 98 99 ❖ RRD 10 9 8 7 6 5 4 3 2 1

Printed and bound in Mexico

Design: Andrew Smith
Page layout and composition: Joseph Gisini, Andrew Smith Graphics, Inc.
Editing: Barbara Schon

ACKNOWLEDGEMENTS
❧

Thanks to all the wonderful gardeners that let photographer Paddy Wales into their
gorgeous gardens: University of British Columbia Botanical Gardens; VanDusen
Botanical Garden; Pamela Frost; Francesca Darts; Valerie Pfeiffer; Audrey Litherland;
Susan Ryley; Peter and Nora Thornton; Lyn Noble; Kathy Leishman; Dick and
Barbara Phillips; Helen and Don Nesbitt; Doris Fancourt–Smith; Ann Buffam; Glen
Patterson; Thomas Hobbs; Karen Morgan.
    And more thanks go to Barbara Schon for her editing skills, and Maya Mavjee at
HarperCollins, who is always on call; to Tom Thomson, Chief Horticulturist at
Humber Nurseries, for reading the manuscript; and to Andrew Smith and Joseph
Gisini for the book design and Tim Saunders for his good ideas.
    The zones indicated in this book follow the United States Department of
Agriculture guide. When there has been conflict over how hardy plants are, I've fol-
lowed the work done by John J. Sabuco, who seems to have more sense than most
people.

COVER: *Viola labradorica*

Contents

Shade Plants

Gardeners often look upon shade as the bane of their gardening lives. It isn't. In fact, a shady area can be one of the most refreshing places in any garden—a blissful contrast to open sunny borders; a mini-woodland that makes a visitor slow down, stop and take a deep breath.

As well, I love shade plants. The many contrasting storeys of plants that can be grown in the shade are astounding. From the tall canopies of old trees, down to minute ground covers; from a profusion of shrubs to the undulating shapes of perennials—this is where I want to spend my time not only gardening but meditating.

In working on the shade section of my garden I had two difficult things to contend with: an old Norway maple on my own property that had been hacked at shamefully, and a gigantic weeping willow in the garden to the south—a tree that I believe should never be planted in a city.

For many years I was discouraged by this area and tended to ignore it. But what changed things and made all the difference was deciding to spend money on regular limbing up of these trees. By removing the lowest branches, more light was let into the whole garden. Slowly I improved the soil by adding what is by now no doubt tons of leaf mold, compost and manure. The soil was slowly raised over the greedy, shallow root systems of these trees. Even in this small space—19' by 40' (6 m by 12 m)—it has taken many years and hundreds of plants to develop a serene glade.

One of my best investments was the help of a professional gardener to install a new design I'd come up with in 1987. It was his idea to make a semicircular berm in this section with the sod that had been uprooted from everywhere else in the garden. It gave a more sculptural form to this little area and makes it far more interesting. The next serious aid was an underground watering system that leaks water through recycled rubber pipes. This is very important for a shade garden. In most cases shade plants prefer moist but not soggy, cool soil, and this system delivers water to the area that needs it—the roots. If you don't have a water source near shady borders you might consider underground hoses.

I also have several indicator plants here: *Petasites japonicus* and *Peltiphyllum peltatum*, both of which have enormous leaves. When they wilt I know I need to put on the watering system or, more likely, water by hand.

Understanding shade is becoming increasingly important. In cities, as the trees get older and more buildings are raised, it's inevitable that we will be dealing with some form of shade. And if we want to cleanse our immediate

*TO IDENTIFY YOUR ZONE, PLEASE SEE THE ZONE CHART ON PAGE 62.

Campanula portenschlagiana with hardy geranium
PHOTOGRAPHED IN THE GARDEN OF: Lyn Noble

environment, we not only have to keep older trees and look after them, we need to plant a lot more young ones.

What confuses most people—it certainly did me when I started this venture—is exactly what kind of shade there is in the garden and how plants respond to it. Gardens have many kinds of shade, and it changes almost every year as a garden matures. Shade gardeners have to be fairly sensitive to local light conditions.

Don't attempt to grow shade plants in the sun; they will burn or have way too many flowers, then wilt pathetically. Look for a spot with the right kind of light and soil for each plant. Save experimenting until your plants have got going, then divide them and have some fun moving them around.

To determine the various *kinds* of shade in your garden, keep track of where the sun is and what sort of shade it's creating at various times of the day.

Here are a couple of shady facts:

꩜ The larger the leaf a plant has, the more likely it will tolerate shade. A large surface is one strategy a plant develops to compensate for low light conditions.

꩜ Moisture content in the air—the humidity that is transpired by the trees around—is extremely important to these plants. An exposed shade garden with a steady wind whipping through will probably need some form of barrier—a windbreak or stand of protective shrubs.

Alchemilla mollis, Lady's Mantle
PHOTOGRAPHED IN THE GARDEN OF: Doris Fancourt–Smith

KINDS OF SHADE

Dappled shade: the ideal is high dappled light provided by trees that filter light through their leaves in a moist atmosphere.

Half shade or semi-shade: at least two hours of sun alternating with shade—morning sun/afternoon shade or morning shade/afternoon sun. This will produce more flowering and reduced leaf size.

Bright light: open to the sky but not to the direct rays of the sun.

Full shade: usually found beneath mature trees, which allow little light through the leaves.

Dense shade: under evergreens and old shrubs; on the north side of a house or garage; between buildings.

There are other variations on shade, but these are the main categories and usually the ones you'll find on plant identification tags. For instance, if a plant is marked "sun/shade", it probably means that the plant can get along in semi-shade.

Keep in mind that heat from the sun intensifies as the day wears on. Thus shade plants exposed to late afternoon sun may suffer somewhat unless they have ideal soil conditions. In spring, the shade section will be fully exposed to sun before the leaves open out on trees and shrubs. And the sun's angle and intensity change with each season.

SOIL

The kind of soil demanded by most shade-loving plants is usually repeated in the listings: light soil with lots of water-retentive humus and good drainage. The ideal is one part sand, one part loamy soil and two parts humus. Since few of us attain this level of perfection, keep adding humus (compost or leaf mold) as side or top dressing around plants. This will slowly break down and help the soil retain moisture and keep cool.

Understanding woodland soil, soil that exists under trees and shrubs, is paramount. Think about a forest—nothing is wasted, and each plant relates to the plant next to it. Obviously, plants of all kinds are going to be competing with the very trees that create the shade in the first place. Composting is crucial. Not a leaf should be removed except to the compost pile or in a separate area, if you have room, where it can break down for next year's leaf mold.

If your shade area is hopelessly filled with surface roots that, if whacked at, might harm the enclosing trees, make slightly raised beds and fill in with the mixture above. If you have solid clay or close-to-the-surface hard-pan, spread this mix on the surface. But don't make the rise more than 6 inches (15 cm). Most perennials and shrubs will be able to make do with this. Any more and you stand to upset the delicate balance that trees live in.

In my own shade section I have what I think is an incredibly efficient double compost bin. The front has removable slats so the compost can regularly be turned with ease. This speeds up decomposition to such an extent that I can get a three-quarters-finished product out in about six weeks. But this does mean turning every few days. When I'm being a real keener, I do it every day. If you don't want to do the work, leave it to break down slowly. It will be ready for the garden in about a year.

Be sure to layer in the compost what you take from the garden (brown—leaves, soil) with what you chop up in the kitchen (green stuff). The smaller the pieces when you put them in the compost, the quicker the material will break down.

I never tidy up the woodland. Again, it's like the forest, which does just fine without people mucking about with rakes and brooms. Lots of leaves stay on the ground, but I brush away by hand any that may create a stifling mat over delicate plants. From my neighbors, I beg as many oak and beech leaves as possible, since they provide acid leaf mold. These I keep in bags with a little soil and store them out of the way because they take so long to disintegrate.

Evergreen cuttings are good mulch around ericaceous plants such as kalmias and pieris, or stacked up as protection from winter blasts. Mulch reduces the chance of a freeze-thaw cycle flinging plants right out of the soil, and keeps the early spring sun from burning them when all the leaves are off the trees. Make something comparable to the duff found on the forest floor: a mixture of pine needles, leaves (chopped up and partly decomposed), compost and manure. Add to the garden once the ground has frozen for winter protection, and then replenish in spring when new growth has started or when it is suggested in the listings.

DESIGNING THE SHADE GARDEN

If you are unfortunate and do not have shade, you can make some by planting trees and shrubs or building structures for vines to grow over. For instance, a lath house or a pergola will cast its own shade. A pergola covered with vines as a walkway between two sections of the garden is an old device and a very good one—plant fast-growing annual vines to provide cover the first year along with slower perennial vines such as *Hydrangea petiolaris* that will take over in the future. One of my favorite shady spots has a small stone bench, cool to sit on, ideally situated to contemplate the plants around.

A shade garden lends itself to informality. Even so, strive for four seasons of interest. That means adding plants with as much size, color and diversity in foliage as possible.

Approach your design in layers or storeys. Consider the shape and color of the foliage of each plant as you place it. Place plants with fine leaves next to those with broad ones for a pleasing contrast; vertical accents are as important as horizontal planes. And look for plants that will echo the soft carpet underfoot in the forest.

GROUND COVERS FOR SHADE

Ajuga pyramidalis, pyramidal bugle flower, zone 2; *A. reptans* 'Burgundy Glow'; *Asarum canadense*, wild ginger, zone 3; *A. caudatum*, British Columbia wild ginger, zone 2; *A. europaeum*, European ginger, zone 5; *Bergenia crassifolia*, leather bergenia, zone 2; *B. cordifolia*, heartleaf bergenia, zone 2; *Cornus canadensis*, bunchberry, zone 3; *Galax aphylla* (syn. *G. urceolata*), galax, zone 3; *Galium odoratum*, sweet woodruff, zone 4; *Gaultheria procumbens*, wintergreen, zone 3; *Lamiastrum galeobdolon* 'Variegatum', yellow archangel, zone 4, does very well in the dry of trees; *Lamium maculatum*, deadnettle, zone 2; *Lysimachia nummularia*, creeping Jenny, zone 3; *Mazus reptans*, mazus, zone 4; *Microbiota decussata*, Siberian carpet cypress, zone 4; *Mitchella repens*, partridge berry, zone 3; *Omphalodes verna*, blue-eyed Mary, zone 5 (see page 44); *Pachysandra procumbens*, Allegheny spurge, zone 3; *Paxistima canbyi* (syn. *Pachistima canbyi*), dwarf mountain lover, rat stripper, zone 3; *Phlox divaricata*, woodland phlox, zone 3; *P. stolonifera*, creeping phlox, zone 3; *Shortia galacifolia*, Oconee-bells, zone 3; *S. soldanelloides* var. *ilicifolia*, Alpenclock shortia; zone 6; *Tiarella cordifolia*, foamflower, zone 3 (see page 55); *Vaccinium crassifolium*, creeping blueberry, zone 5;

V. vitis-idaea var. *minus*, lingonberry, mountain cranberry, zone 2; *Vancouveria*, barrenwort, zone 4; *Vinca minor*, periwinkle, myrtle, zone 2; *Waldsteinia fragarioides*, barren strawberry, zone 2; *W. ternata*, zone 3.

SHADE PESTS

Garden enemy number one is The Slug. They love a cool, moist atmosphere and munching on all those luscious large-leaved plants. Here's a good old-fashioned remedy:

Add 1 tsp (15 mL) each of brewer's yeast, sweetener (honey or molasses) and vegetable oil to a 16 oz (500 g) yogurt container of water. Set it into the ground with the rim at soil level and collect the dead each day. I use this method, but when all is said and done, the most effective way to deal with slugs is to pick by hand early in the morning or as the light is beginning to fade in early evening. There are commercial slug baits, but I steer clear of them mainly because most warn about being dangerous to children, pets and birds—all of which I welcome into the garden.

Specific pests are mentioned in the listings. Woodlands generally seem to take very good care of themselves if the planting is sensitive and the mix is one that will make the trees and shrubs comfortable and doesn't disturb delicate root systems. The plants suggested here are mainly perennials. You will find many more shade-loving plants in *Favorite Flowering Shrubs* and *Favorite Annuals*.

Milium effusum 'Aureum' with *Kiftsgate rose*
PHOTOGRAPHED IN: VanDusen Botanical Garden

Aconitum henryi

FAMILY NAME: *Ranunculaceae* / ZONE: 2
PHOTOGRAPHED IN: University of British Columbia Botanical Gardens

The peculiar brooding quality of aconitums explains, in part, why these marvellous plants have ended up with such strange common names. They have also become the stuff of many tales because all parts are poisonous. You would never put this plant near vegetables or a children's garden.

A. *napellus* is an even more poisonous plant in the wild than under cultivation. It contains aconitina, one of the most deadly of all poisons. The tiniest dose may paralyze a victim or prove fatal through asphyxiation. Whenever you handle this plant, be sure to wash your hands afterwards.

Margery Fish, the great English shade gardener, says this is the best of all perennials for shade. It will also grow in some sun, which makes it a useful vertical plant for almost anywhere in the garden. Use it at the edges of a shade section, one with dappled light.

A member of the buttercup family, there are either 100 or 350 species in the genus, depending on your source. They are native to Europe and Asia and any mountainous area of the Northern Hemisphere. It is a herbaceous, clump-forming plant with long, thick, tuberous-shaped roots. There is even a vine form, which I like very much.

The most fascinating part of the plant is the flowers, with their stiff little hooded helmets emerging in midsummer through fall in deep, deep blues and purples, white, ivory and yellow. They grow straight above the lobed foliage in erect racemes or panicles (flower clusters).

Aconitum henryi, a native of China, zone 4, has slender branched stems.

PLANTING & MAINTENANCE TIPS

❧ This plant prefers somewhat moist soil with lots of added humus. The warmer the region, the more shade needed. Generally speaking, it doesn't like to be disturbed, but can be moved by digging down deeply to get the long tap root, or dividing it up if necessary. Take a lot of soil with the root.

❧ Add manure and compost to fertilize in spring; mulch to keep weeds down.

Aconitum henryi

It grows from 3' – 5' (1 m – 1.5 m) with a spread of about 2 feet (60 cm). The dark blue flowers rise over deeply notched leaves. *A. h.* 'Sparks Variety' has slender, tapering stems; blooms in July. An easy plant, and if, for some reason, you can't grow delphiniums successfully, try aconitums to get a similar elongated shape and color.

A handsome plant that provides excellent height in a shady border or works as a drift of blue in an area of high dappled light. It is a sensational cut flower—and dried as well. Cut off the blooms when they are about to open and hang them upside down for two weeks.

OTHER SPECIES & CULTIVARS

A. carmichaelii, a native of China, grows to 2' – 5' (60 cm – 1.5 m); flowers wand-like panicles 8 inches (20 cm) long in blue or white; zone 2.

A. napellus is broader than it is tall, with leafy stems; grows 3' – 4' (1 m – 1.2 m) tall, with hairy leaves 2" – 4" (5 cm – 10 cm) divided into three parts. It spreads 2' – 3' (60 cm – 1 m) and doesn't need staking. This is the most commonly available; zone 2.

'Bressingham Spire', deep violet-blue flowers, dark green foliage, to 3 feet (1 m).

A. x *bicolor*, blue flower spikes with a frosting of white in late summer; grows to 3 feet (1 m); zone 4; in colder areas use a heavy mulch.

A. septentrionale 'Ivorine', exceptional monkshood; white flowers in summer.

Adiantum pedatum

FAMILY NAME: *Polypodiaceae* / ZONE: 2
PHOTOGRAPHED IN THE GARDEN OF: Lyn Noble

A ny shade garden demands ferns. Each region has at least one ubiquitous
fern that will volunteer whether you want it or not. They are magnificent to cover up all the detritus left behind by spring bulbs.

If you can grow ferns, *Adiantum pedatum*, maidenhair fern, is a beauty.
It is just one of more than 200 species of ferns native to North America. It
grows to 18 inches (45 cm) with a spread of about 12 inches (30 cm). The
young fronds are pink, eventually turning black. This particular fern must
have moist, loose soil to make large colonies. It will take just about any
kind of soil under light shade.

Most ferns must have a steady source of moisture. They are primitive
plants that never developed sophisticated strategies to keep from drying
out. They must also have shade and like a comfortable humid atmosphere.

Adiantum pedatum

Having said that, there are also a few ferns that will grow in dry shade: *Asplenium platyneuron*, ebony spleenwort; *Athyrium filix-femina*, lady fern; *Dryopteris filix-mas* 'Cristata', crested male fern. All need water, however, when they start developing fronds in spring.

Ferns are incredibly useful plants. They will mask the bare legs of old rhodos and azaleas; they can make the transition from one section of the garden to the next; and are attractive with most other woodland or shade plants. Here are some of the things I plant among ferns: *Sanguinaria canadensis*, bloodroot; *Cypripedium acaule*, Lady's slipper; *Actaea pachypoda*, white baneberry; *Caulophyllum thalictroides*, blue cohosh; and medium-sized hostas that won't overwhelm them.

PLANTING & MAINTENANCE TIPS

❧ General fern care: Most ferns can take an acid to neutral or alkaline site under light shade; moisture is important for most, but some do just fine in dry shade.

❧ Make sure you give ferns a mulch of leaves before it snows. You might have to use a light plastic netting edged with bricks to keep the leaves from blowing all over the place. Not very foresty looking, but useful nevertheless.

OTHER SPECIES & CULTIVARS

Athyrium goeringianum 'Pictum' has silver-bronze and metallic fronds; an excellent pot or edging plant. Also listed as *A. isaneanum pictum*. Zone 6.

Dryopteris filix-mas is one of the few ferns for dry shade, though it needs a good moist start each year. Native to Europe and North America, it's spectacular, with fronds as wide as 1½ feet (45 cm). Barnesii is a good cultivar. Zone 3.

Osmunda cinnamomea, cinnamon fern, is eaten as fiddleheads; grows up to 6 feet (2 m) in the wild and looks almost prehistoric; in a garden it is about half that size; zone 3.

O. claytoniana, interrupted fern, has deeply cut, coarse pinnae; deciduous; doesn't spread rapidly; zone 3.

O. regalis, Royal fern, is like a humongous maidenhair; will not tolerate dry shade; zone 2.

Polystichum acrostichoides, Christmas fern, survives severe winters, grows 2' – 3' (60 – 90 cm) and needs moist soil. The new growth of the 5–inch (12.5 cm) wide fronds is almost vertical while the previous year's growth is horizontal; zone 3.

Matteuccia pensylvanica, Ostrich fern, can just about be grown in a bog. This huge vase-shaped plant can reach 6 feet (2 m). Also listed as *M. struthiopteris*. Zone 3.

Alchemilla mollis

FAMILY NAME: *Rosaceae* / ZONE: 3
PHOTOGRAPHED IN THE GARDEN OF: Pamela Frost

*A*lchemilla mollis (syn. *A. vulgaris*), Lady's mantle, is my favorite perennial. It works in sun as well as shade. It's a plant that reproduces without pollination (apomixis) and will spread relentlessly if you let it go to seed. That, however, makes it a successful ground cover. It's the best of all plants to use as an edger, softening paths and brick walkways, and filling out the most boring of places. And this enchanting plant has the ability to hold the last drop of dew in the centre of its velvety scalloped leaves.

It's considered invasive, but severe deadheading will keep it in check. A few babies, however, will spring up even if you don't let it go to seed. They are easy to pull out and even better to transplant. It takes a couple of years before they hit mature size.

If you have problems with an eroding slope, alchemillas will hold soil in place. Even better, they are useful as a ground cover because weeds just can't get through its tough thick roots.

In the sun it can grow to a fair height, almost 2 feet (60 cm). But in the shade this little beauty stays comfortably in place at about 1 foot (30 cm). The gray-green leaves grow to about 2" – 6" (5 cm – 15 cm). Soft and sensuous to the touch, they combine extremely well with lots of other plants.

The acid yellow flowers are not wildly interesting unless you do the following: just as they get to the very fullest almost frothy stage but well before turning brownish in seed, cut them off right at ground level. Hang the flowers upside down in a cool, dark place for a couple of weeks. They dry out magnificently for dried flower arrangements. They are also a long-lasting attractive addition to any fresh bouquet.

I like to see the early spring bulbs pushing up against the ratty-looking alchemilla mounds left by winter's devastation. Then the alchemilla emerges—delicate pale, pale green to cover up the dying foliage of bulbs.

Use it to knit one group of plants with another, for instance next to *Helichrysum petiolatum* and an artemisia; or along with a ground cover such as *Lysimachia nummularia*, creeping Jenny, which also has a bright yellow flower and blooms at the same time; or as a contrast with tall vertical plants such as aconitums or Japanese anemones.

❧ Plant in a cool, moist, but not overly wet, soil. Under the right condition of semi-shade, any kind of soil will do. Blooming will last longer in moist rather than dry soil. If you decide to grow alchemillas in the sun, make sure there is some protection from blazing noon rays. I like to chop each plant right back to the newest little growth near the base once it starts looking a bit sorry for itself. It won't look like much for a week but then will come back renewed and gorgeous.

❧ To add to your stock of alchemillas, let at least one plant go to seed and you'll find the minute babies all over the place. Once they get to be about an inch (1.5 cm) high, dig them up and put them where you want them. You can do this just about any time of the year.

Since hybrid tea roses look rather leggy, these plants work well in masking them as they do with big old rhododendrons. Experiment with such wonderful combinations as this contrast in colors—*Heuchera sanguinea* 'Palace Purple', or next to *Liriope muscari* 'Variegata'.

OTHER SPECIES & CULTIVARS

A. x *splendens* doesn't spread as quickly or easily; the leaves have the slightest white trim and the flowers are smaller. Good for the rock garden.

Alchemilla mollis
with *Lysimachia
nummularia*
'Aurea'

Astilbe x arendsii
'Bridal Veil'

FAMILY NAME: *Saxifragaceae* / ZONE: 3
PHOTOGRAPHED IN THE GARDEN OF: Francesca Darts

I have astilbes in a border along a sheltering fence near the house. This hardy herbaceous plant will bring clouds of color—in a range that includes rose, pink, salmon, peach, bright crimson, lilac, mauve—to any shady spot during the summer months. In bloom, they are glorious puffs of colored smoke. And by not cutting them back in the fall, the plumed seedheads make sculptural forms against the snows of winter.

The plumes (called panicles) are actually myriad tiny florets. They are very sensual when in bloom and can almost double the size of the plant. They add a kind of texture to the shady border not seen in any other plant. But it's the deeply cut leaves that I find so appealing. The bronze to bright green foliage has an airy quality that lightens up dense plantings considerably.

Astilbes come in a wide variety of sizes, from curious little ground covers to fine vertical plants with stems up to 2 feet (60 cm) high. With some planning, it's possible to have astilbes in bloom from June through September by planting species and cultivars with successive blooming times. In warmer regions, the plant will bloom even earlier.

A. x arendsii 'Bridal Veil' is one of the finest of all the hybrids in this interesting group of plants. With pure white plumes, it grows 2' – 4' (60 cm – 1.2 m) high and about the same across.

Astilbes do best in partial shade but must have good air circulation. I had some too close to a densely constructed north-facing fence. They were not happy until moved away from the fence and then they perked right up.

In the country garden, they enhance the edge of a stream or pond and can be used to create drifts of color to demarcate the transition into a shade or woodland garden. They grow successfully under trees and near shrubs.

They make great cut flowers, or dry them upside down in a cool place. Within a few weeks they are ready to be put in a dried arrangement. I usually leave most of the plants alone because their erect seedheads look so good in winter.

I like to plant lots of the smaller early spring bulbs such as scillas and snowdrops around them so that the emerging foliage can cover up any

Astilbe 'Bridal Veil', with A. *simplicifolia* 'Sprite'

bulb mess left behind. In another spot I have variegated tulips that come out fairly late in the season. The astilbes overshadow them when the leaves start looking limp and nasty. I also combine them with various kinds of lilies; some bloom before the astilbes and others bloom later in the season. *Cimicifuga*, snakeroot; *Anemone japonica*, Japanese anemone; and hardy geraniums make an attractive threesome that doesn't take up a lot of room in a small garden.

The foliage of astilbes and hellebores makes a good marriage of contrasts—the smooth edges and deeper color of the hellebores contrasting with the lighter but deeply notched leaves of the astilbe. Another combination that looks great: astilbe and iris. When the iris finish, the astilbe come into their own.

PLANTING & MAINTENANCE TIPS

❦ This plant can take some neglect, and tolerates light to deeper shade. The soil should be moist, especially during hot weather—if they look like they are about to fall over, they probably are. I grow mine in clay soil where the drainage isn't perfect, and I don't worry about watering them as often as those in the woodland area, which has much sharper drainage. Allowing them to dry out too often shortens the longevity of what should be easy, long-lived plants.

❦ During especially cold years, when temperatures go down to –30°F (–35°C), there might be some winterkill, but the plant will come back in spring, though perhaps later than usual.

❦ Add lots of organic matter to the soil (good for holding in water anyway)—well-rotted manure, compost, finely shredded bark.

❦ For successful planting, keep the crown at the surface of the soil and water well immediately. Usually leave about 2 feet (60 cm) between plants.

❦ Feed with compost and manure a couple of times a year and mulch around the plants away from the crowns.

❦ Divide by cutting the carrot-textured crown into wedges with a butcher knife anytime, even when in plume.

OTHER SPECIES & CULTIVARS

A. x *arendsii* 'Cattleya' has rose-pink flowers; 'Ostrich Plume', pink, cascading flowers; 'Spartan', deep red.

A. chinensis 'Pumila' is a dwarf form excellent for all climates; grows 8" – 18" (20 cm – 45 cm) wide; a good stoloniferous ground cover with attractive foliage. Unless you plant carefully, however, it can look a bit ditzy with all these little pink candles sticking up all over the place. It's about the easiest of the astilbes to grow. I have mine in a spot that can get fairly dry, and though it doesn't spread readily, it is still very healthy.

A. simplicifolia 'Sprite' grows 8" – 15" (20 cm – 38 cm); good for the rock garden or as ground cover. Late-season bloom for these little guys. Gorgeous foliage.

A. var. *davidii* has low foliage; reedy flower stem grows to 6 feet (2 m); blue-anthered lavender flowers; does well in moist or dryish soil; flowers in full shade (prefers part); doesn't like being divided; grows from seed.

A. taquetii, late astilbe; grows to 3'– 4' (1 m – 1.2 m) with leaves 4" – 6" (10 cm – 15 cm) long. Similar to *A. chinensis* but taller and more tolerant of dry conditions; glorious magenta; blooms in July. Zone 4.

'Superba', tall, slender midseason bloomer with lavender-pink plumes.

Campanula lactiflora

FAMILY NAME: *Campanulaceae* / ZONE: 5; 3 to 9, depending on the species
PHOTOGRAPHED IN THE GARDEN OF: Kathy Leishman
and the University of British Columbia Botanical Gardens

C ampanulas are a passion. This genus is so gratifying I'd recommend collecting them. There are at least 300 species, and the colors are rich whites, blues and purples. The elegance of the cup- and bell-shaped flowers has long fascinated gardeners. You can put them in sunny borders or rock and scree gardens, and, best of all, many of them prefer the shade.

These Mediterranean and Northern Hemisphere plants are herbaceous, with woody roots and basal leaves (leaves at the base of the plant); they are very efficient seeders. If you need a plant to fill in glaring holes, look to this family. The sizes range from a miniscule 1 inch (2.5 cm) to at least 6 feet (2 m), sometimes even more depending on the species.

The leaves come in many forms: heart- or lance-shaped, oval, some are notched, some are toothed at the margins. There is such a dazzling array of

Campanula lactiflora

Campanula carpatica 'White Clips'

campanulas, I have them all over my garden.

Combine plants with relatives in the same family, for example *Platycodon*, balloon flower; *Symphyandra*; *Phyteuma*, Horned rampion. I have *C. persicifolia* combined with the latter because the blue and white forms of these plants are particularly harmonious.

C. lactiflora, milky bellflower, can grow into a 6–foot (2 m) monster, but it's a superb tough, long-living plant that can survive dry spots even in less than satisfactory soil and shade. The sprays of palest blue blooms repeat themselves if they are deadheaded; simply cut back to just below the flowers. Keep the attractive foliage intact. If you don't deadhead, expect to find seeds all over the place. It might need staking.

'Loddon Anna' is a pink form; 'Alba' is pure white.

C. lactiflora looks wonderful with other tall plants such as lilies, phlox and *Lysimachia clethroides*, Gooseneck Loostrife, which is also white and blooms at the same time.

There are campanulas perfect for the woodland garden. Use *C. alliariifolia* as a transition between grass and open woodland. Others are good as edging for paths if it isn't too shady. Work them in among rhododendrons and other plants that enjoy high light shade.

Some campanulas are in the weed class. *C. rapunculoides*, creeping bellflower, has become such a nuisance that it's been declared a noxious weed in Manitoba and a nuisance weed in Alberta. In other regions there's enough competition to keep this one at bay. In vacant lots it thrives.

❧ Light shade to full sunlight will accommodate this plant. Most campanulas need well-drained soil. And, I've found to my dismay, when there's been a winter with them sitting in damp that turns to ice, they will croak.

❧ Add a little bone meal to the soil occasionally. And always cut them back after flowering if you don't want them seeding about.

❧ I've never found anything except slugs to take to this plant. And hand picking is the method I've always used. Some mornings my 'White Clips' are sticky with them. Consider this a trap plant, and come with the slug-stomping slippers.

OTHER SPECIES & CULTIVARS

C. alliariifolia has small white bells.

C. carpatica, Carpathian bellflower, forms a spreading clump, with branching stems and bright green oval leaves. *C. c.* 'White Clips', grows 18" by 18" (45 cm by 45 cm). 'Blue Clips', of course, is the blue form. It grows in clumps with bright green oval leaves that become more heart-shaped as they go up the stem. Needs sun.

C. cochleariifolia; the flowers are little shell-like ears, as the name implies. It will seed itself all over a rock wall around patio stones and, more slowly, in and around the edge of the shade garden. It has been described as a joyous plant, and I'd go along with that. It creeps along on rhizomes even in the worst of all possible situations, which is where I've got it. It doesn't spread quickly in dry shade competing with lots of other plants.

C. glomerata, clustered bellflower, purple flowers, grows in sun or part shade, 1' – 3' (30 cm – 90 cm), known as 'Dane's Blood'; zone 3.

C. latifolia also likes shade. Erect unbranched stems grow up to 4 feet (1.2 m) with purple-blue flowers; zone 3. 'Alba' is a white form. 'Macrantha' has dark blue, almost purple flowers.

C. persicifolia, willow or peach-leaved bellflower, grows in dry shade to 2' – 3' (60 cm – 1 m), with flowers that hang down elegantly along vertical stems from basal rosettes of round-toothed leaves. Daily deadheading keeps this one in bloom for months. Self-seeds if you allow it and produces variants in the blooms ranging from white to dark blue. 'Alba', white. 'Telham Beauty', light blue; zone 3.

C. poscharskyana grows in just about any climate; divide to make a gorgeous ground cover; violet star-like flowers. When it starts to flop over, cut back. It will flower in almost full shade and take dry spells with great tolerance. Zone 3.

C. portenschlagiana, Dalmation bellflower; spreads with the rapaciousness of any good ground cover. It has heart-shaped leaves, brilliant blue funnel-shaped flowers. Grows 6" – 9" (15 cm – 22 cm) high. Longer flowering than the above; zone 4.

C. rotundifolia, English harebell, bluebells-of-Scotland, is really a native of North America. Good in part shade. Flowers all summer long. *C. r.* var. *alba*, white. Zone 3.

Cimicifuga simplex ramosa 'Atropurpurea'

FAMILY NAME: *Ranunculaceae* / ZONE: 4
PHOTOGRAPHED IN THE GARDEN OF: Francesca Darts

C imicifuga is an imposing, rather tall, clumping creature. The white
plumes of the late-blooming flowers almost glow in a shady part of the
garden. But this adaptable plant can take sun as well. *C. simplex ramosa*
'Atropurpurea' is one of my favorites and it grows in both sun and shade.
The more sun, the darker the foliage. Grows to 5 feet (1.5 m) high, 3 foot
(90 cm) spread. It has deeply notched foliage, broadly cut leaves on stiff but
gracefully bending stems. The bottlebrush white flowers are the latest of all

Cimicifuga ramosa

PLANTING & MAINTENANCE TIPS

❧ They thrive in deep, well-drained, cool, moist soil with lots of organic matter. Need part shade. They never need staking, nor have I seen any pests on them.

❧ They can be divided in spring before new growth begins, but be careful and make sure you get a good clean cut. Make sure that each division has at least two eyes and that the rhizome is planted $1\frac{1}{2}$ inches (4 cm) below the surface, 2 feet (60 cm) apart.

❧ If you have the patience to start these plants from seed, chill them for several weeks in the fridge. Germination might be slow or erratic.

❧ The farther south you are, the heavier the shade they will tolerate. In too much sun they will eventually burn.

the cimicifugas to open up. 'Brunette' is a new cultivar with the deepest hue and the biggest price.

The flowers look like showers of infinitely tiny stars floating over the top of the plant. As soon as they open up from the bottom, they fall away. Then green seedheads develop that last and last.

A drift of cimicifugas is marvellous on its own, but I like to see them mixed in with other simple tall plants, such as *Lilium regale,* or *Thalictrum rochebrunianum* with its blue foliage and almost purple flowers. The latter blooms in spring and the *C. simplex* from September to October.

Bugbanes add an almost weightless quality to the edge of an open woodland garden. They also echo the shape of such shrubs as *Cotoneaster dielsianus,* which shares its graceful arching shape. Another plant I combine with it is *Viburnum tomentosum* 'Summer Snowflake'. And, since the leaves resemble each other, astilbes make another harmonious arrangement. As do ferns, daylilies and *Boltonia asteroides.*

Another of my favorite garden compositions is *C. s.* 'White Pearl' and 'Atropurpurea' together with the pink and white forms of *Anemone japonica.* All bloom at the end of August and into September. They are ravishing.

OTHER SPECIES & VARIETIES

C. racemosa, black snakeroot, native to eastern North America, has black stems with white flowers, deep green foliage; grows to 7 feet (2 m); sun/shade; zone 3.

C. r. var. *cordifolia* is slighter coarser in texture than the above; scented white flowers bloom in midsummer.

C. simplex 'White Pearl', sometimes called 'The Pearl', has large white bottlebrushes with green fruits; grows 3' – 4' (1 m – 1.2 m), zone 3.

Dicentra formosa
'Luxuriant'

FAMILY NAME: *Fumariaceae* / ZONE: 2 (best in cooler zones)
PHOTOGRAPHED IN: University of British Columbia Botanical Gardens

No garden seems complete without a bleeding heart. We all grew up with the huge blowsy plants bearing the standard valentines hanging along each stalk; there are now many interesting species and cultivars available. One explanation for its widespread use is that dicentras are native to North America (as well as parts of Asia and the Himalayas).

I'm crazy about these plants not only because they have long-lasting blooms but because the foliage has an almost fern-like quality. The heart-shaped flowers grow in racemes or panicles above the foliage; the corolla has two outer and two inner pouch-shaped petals.

PLANTING & MAINTENANCE TIPS

❧ Excellent for partial or full shade; light but moist woodland soil that doesn't dry out will make this plant thrive. It needs well-drained soil and won't survive in ground that remains wet. I can attest to this. My garden floods every spring, and only one little *Dicentra eximia* withstands the onslaught. Prefers the shade, of course, especially in warmer areas. Needs the cold to give it a good long winter rest.

❧ Some species spread by tubers, others with rhizotomous roots—these are much slower.

❧ If you decide to grow this plant in the sun, the foliage will disappear once the flowers have bloomed. The big old species will spread their babies all over the place unless you deadhead seriously.

❧ They last for years, as we see from the ancient plants in old gardens, but they do much better if divided up about every four years. The roots are extremely brittle, so be careful how you handle them. Transplant each root with an eye (bud) and a root piece that is at least 2 inches (10 cm). They need lots and lots of top dressing with a combination of compost, leaf mold and manure. Leave about 2 feet (60 cm) between plants.

Dicentra formosa 'Luxuriant'

Dicentra eximia, fringed bleeding heart, is a small 9" – 12" (22 cm – 30 cm) plant with flowers coming and going most of the summer. Even when the locket-shaped flowers have disappeared, the gray-blue basal foliage is attractive on its own.

D. formosa 'Luxuriant' is probably my favorite hybrid, and it blooms in waves from June until the end of the season. The deeply incised leaves and purple-red flowers can take sun. They make good cut flowers and it doesn't spread about. I've had years when it comes back later in the season. When the foliage starts to fade it goes a mucky yellow and just disappears.

For felicitous combinations, use *Dicentra* with plants of similar foliage such as *Corydalis lutea* with its gray leaves and yellow flowers; grows 12" – 15" (30 cm – 38 cm); *corydalis* is a frantic self-seeder, be careful where you put it. Also attractive with some of the old-fashioned peonies (the big floppy ones).

OTHER SPECIES & CULTIVARS

D. cucullaria, Dutchman's-breeches, a native of North America, flowers in early spring, then the basal leaves die back.

D. formosa grows to 18 inches (45 cm) with dainty ferny foliage and deep pink heart-shaped blooms; expands by underground stolons and makes a good carpet; native to western North America.

'Alba', light green leaves; flowers are white nodding sprays.

'Adrian Bloom' has profuse crimson flowers.

D. spectabilis is the bleeding heart of childhood memories, with the big red-and-white hearts dangling from long branches; prefers half shade. 'Alba', white, 3' (1 m).

Epimedium × youngianum

FAMILY NAME: Berberidaceae / ZONE: 4 to 8
PHOTOGRAPHED IN THE GARDEN OF: Lyn Noble

Epimediums are the classic shade plant. No woodland garden is worthy of the name without them. The nodding leaves in the shape of a heart or a shield seem delicate, yet they are tough and easy to grow.

The family comes from Asia, along with species native to areas around the Mediterranean. The famous plant hunter Phillip Franz van Siebold (after whom all plants with *sieboldii* are named) brought several to Europe in the nineteenth century.

Epimedium × *youngianum*

PLANTING & MAINTENANCE TIPS

❧ Don't cut them back in fall and they will keep their spindly-looking branches all winter long.

❧ Epimediums thrive in the light shade of other acid-loving plants and in moist humusy soil, slightly acid and well drained. They will tolerate some dry shade.

❧ Some grow by stolons travelling underground, rooting as they go along, others by rhizomes (underground horizontal stems).

❧ Divide in spring while still dormant or after foliage matures. Lift them and cut in two or into wedges with a large strong knife.

❧ In late winter cut back dead foliage of deciduous and semi-evergreen species to expose new growth.

Epimediums are the perfect plants to combine with any fern. At first, they grow very, very slowly; don't plant them too close to each other or to anything else for that matter—once established, they will reach maximum size very quickly. This is one of the few ground-covering shade plants. You can camouflage a substantial area of barren ground with these plants for a really marvellous effect.

Epimedium x *youngianum*, Young's barrenwort, grows to 6" – 8" (15 cm – 20 cm) high. The foliage is among the loveliest of all woodland plants.

'Niveum', compact form with white flowers.

'Rose Queen', deep pink flowers, spurs tipped white, very showy form.

Epimediums grow well around the base of trees. It accepts the shade of shrubs and other plants such as *Podophyllum peltatum*, may apple.

OTHER SPECIES & VARIETIES

E. grandiflorum, Bishop's hat, a long-spur epimedium, is the most widely cultivated form; violet-crimson flowers. A good plant to hold soil in place.

'Violaceum' has light violet petals.

x *rubrum*, grows 12" – 14" (30 cm – 35 cm); good spreader with strong leaf color that starts as pale coral, then warms up to an orangy red before turning green; red and yellow flowers. This one is considered choice. A great one with the blue hostas.

x *versicolor* 'Sulphureum', inner sepals are pale yellow, petals brighter yellow.

Erythronium tuolumnense

FAMILY NAME: *Liliaceae* / ZONE: 5
PHOTOGRAPHED IN: VanDusen Botanical Garden

Erythronium tuolumnense with *E. oregonum*

A native plant of such splendor it seems almost an exotic, but it grows all over North America. Walking in March or early April and coming upon a naturalized swathe of these glorious plants is enough to make you catch your breath in sheer pleasure.

The most common of these members of the lily family are called dogtooth violets. They look more like cyclamens than violets with their nodding lily-like flowers. They have a delicate scent that fits perfectly with the graceful stance these plants take. The flowers come early and disappear once bloom is over.

E. dens-canis, the dogtooth violet, is a European and Asian species grown for the flowers, which hang down over leaves mottled in reddish brown. This easy-to-grow perennial will take any dappled light right up to full shade. Grows to 6 inches (15 cm) and has rose to purple flowers. Blooms in most areas in April for a few weeks. It does, however, take several years to establish.

There are two usual explanations for the "dogtooth" business. One is that the roots are shaped like canine teeth, the other is that the name refers to the pointy white corms. Either way, it's a terrible name for such an elegant flower.

'Lilac Wonder' has large lilac flowers.

'White Splendor', the largest of all, has pure white flowers.

Even the western erythroniums shown here are adaptable to other places in North America. *Erythronium tuolumnense*, though it is a California native, grows and reproduces itself with great ease almost anywhere. Grows to 1 foot (30 cm); shiny green leaves with yellow flowers.

I have little clusters of erythroniums under a *Cornus alba* 'Sibirica' that bridges the gap between the flowering of that shrub and the rise of the hostas that surround them. They also give pleasure in more obvious places, such as edging a woodland path or dancing under a birch tree along with *Viola labradorica*.

OTHER SPECIES & CULTIVARS

E. americanum, Trout Lily from Nova Scotia and south; yellow flowers and mottled leaves; zone 3.

E. californicum has strongly mottled leaves; creamy white lily-like flowers; grows 10" – 12" (25 cm – 30 cm).

'Pagoda' grows 15" – 18" (38 cm – 45 cm) with branching yellow flowers.

'White Beauty' has cream-colored flowers; tongue-shaped mottled leaves

E. oregonum, a West Coast native; white to cream flowers; grows to 1 foot (30 cm).

PLANTING & MAINTENANCE TIPS

❧ Prefers the cool climate of a woodland with moist, well-drained soil rich in leaf mold. Plant the bulbs about 3" (7 cm) deep. The thin end of the corm should face up.

❧ Divide or increase by offsets in fall. The corms cluster beneath the soil when the leaves die away; lift them when the leaves are dead. Don't let them dry out before replanting.

❧ Can be naturalized in grass since all evidence will be gone by June with only seedpods left.

Geranium x 'Johnson's Blue'

FAMILY NAME: *Geraniaceae* / ZONE: 4
PHOTOGRAPHED IN THE GARDEN OF: Peter and Nora Thornton

Hardy geraniums have a special place in my heart. They were the first flowers—blue yet—to grow in my shady borders. The plants that are usually called geraniums are *Pelargonium*, tender plants from South Africa. Hardy geraniums are a completely different species in the same family. They are mostly herbaceous perennials, though in warmer areas some remain evergreen all winter.

Hardy geraniums are probably the most flexible plants you'll ever bring into the garden. From small ground-hugging buns to spreading mounds and tall slender plants

in need of staking, there are worthwhile geraniums for your garden.

The low-growing forms can course about the feet of larger geraniums; the medium and large ones look magnificent grown with roses to cover up their naked legs. The sun lovers look particularly good next to artemisias, whose silver foliage is a dramatic contrast to the deep green cut leaves of the geraniums. Low-mounding versions set among any of the perennials in the garden fill in blanks left by bulbs or other perennials that have seen their best.

There are 300 to 400 species and cultivars; at least 150 are grown in North America. The cranesbill dubbing comes from the shape of the seed. The foliage is as handsome as any you'll find. The leaves come in a variety of shapes, colors and textures, some fine, some rather coarse. The enchanting flowers have five petals and come in white, pink, magenta, blue and purple.

It really is possible to have a geranium in bloom or at least doing something interesting from early spring to autumn. They don't need much care apart from deadheading. Garden pests leave them alone. What a bonus!

G. x 'Johnson's Blue' is one of the very best of all the hybrids. The 2–inch (5 cm) blue flowers put on a dazzling show for months. Its 2–foot (60 cm) height makes it an ideal plant to combine with others in the same scale.

The abundant light blue flowers work especially well with pale Asiatic lilies that bloom at the same time.

Another good marriage is between peonies and geraniums—when the blooms of peonies fade, the geraniums take over. They look quite at home with *Stachys*, lamb's ears, and any of the veronicas.

Some, such as *G. maculatum*, which has both a pink and a white form, can often be found

Geranium
x 'Johnson's Blue'

growing in the wild. This is a tough one for midshade and will pop up in cracks in stone and along rivers. The ideal one for a country garden or companions with shrubs in a mixed border.

Experimenting with geraniums is easy since they take little care and can be divided up and spread around. Finding any pink or blue flower growing in a shady area is always sheer delight.

PLANTING & MAINTENANCE TIPS

❧ Hardy geraniums like fairly ordinary garden soil. Check each variety to find out its sun requirements. Some thrive in a light shade, others in anything up to full sun.

❧ Divide them up almost any time and spread them around. Cut back after flowering almost to the ground (you'll see where new growth is starting) and they will bloom a second time.

OTHER SPECIES & CULTIVARS

This is only a short list of the plants available from nurseries.

G. endressii, a native of the Pyrenees, has silver-pink funnel-shaped flowers with slight striations of red; grows 18 inches (45 cm) high.

'Wargrave Pink', pale salmon pink that will rebloom if it's cut right back to the ground after flowering. Deeply divided light green leaves.

G. macrorrhizum spreads all over shady areas, therefore is the perfect nurse plant—moving in and filling exposed ground. The magenta blooms are small, but the foliage has a wonderful scent and turns vivid scarlet in fall.

'Ingwersen's Variety', a very attractive clear pink bloom.

G. m. album is a white form that lights up a dark section.

G. pratense has violet flowers tinged with purple, white and lavender; grows to 3 feet (1 m). There are tons of cultivars in this group.

G. psilostemon, Armenian cranesbill, grows to 4 feet (1.2 m) high and just about as wide, so make sure you have room for this incredible plant. The flowers (it's very floriferous, as they say in the biz) are magenta with a strong blue in them. Can be really difficult to combine with other plants, but who cares. Keep out of midday sun, up to partial shade; zone 5.

Helleborus argutifolius

FAMILY NAME: *Ranunculaceae* / ZONE: 4
PHOTOGRAPHED IN THE GARDEN OF: Lyn Noble

I was astounded the first time a hellebore bloomed in my garden. I'd planted it in the shady section and one day noticed a flash of luminous white amid the mud of spring. I was so enchanted that I made visiting friends slog out to get a better view.

I planted *Helleborus niger*, Christmas rose, mainly because I liked the dense green leaves and the fact that they will spread. That they might bloom was sheer serendipity. Under a birch tree they look as though they'd been invented for the site along with *Sanguinaria canadensis*, bloodroot.

Hellebores are among the first and the last to bloom, depending how

Helleborus argutifolius

cold your winters are. In warm areas there are hellebores that bloom in early winter; in colder areas early spring. *H. niger*, the Christmas rose, flowers around the end of February or in March, and the colder the area, the later in the season.

The pendant bell-shaped flowers have the peculiar habit of hanging face out inquisitively. The form is very interesting, with five large overlapping sepals in white, green or purple. This plant is protogynous: the stigmas reach maturity before the stamens, so cross-pollination takes place very easily and in a later stage they are self-pollinating.

H. lividus has spiny-toothed leaves with semi-woody stems; pale green flowers, which are quite startling the first time you see them; grows to 4 feet (1.2 m). With this species, avoid a lot of damp or much drought. They can get leggy in deep shade. It takes about three years from seed to flower. Be sure to plant seedlings in permanent places when they are very young.

H. orientalis, Lenten rose, is the easiest of the hellebores to grow partly because it self-seeds all over the place. It has many flowers, is hardy and long-lived and can take just about any soil. It doesn't like it too hot or dry in summer and certainly not wet in winter. Some seeds are airborne, others may be

PLANTING & MAINTENANCE TIPS

❧ All hellebores like neutral, well-drained soil. The normal woodland conditions that they like—shady, cool and moist—are usually more on the acid side of the pH scale. Rather than add lime to neutralize the soil, let the plants adjust to the area. Make sure plenty of leaf mold and compost are added to the top of the soil. Never plant too deeply—the crown should be no more than 1 inch (2.5 cm) below the surface. Deep planting keeps it from flowering well. The roots are very brittle, so be careful when you're handling them.

❧ Needs generous lashings of compost and leaf mold to feed greedy roots.

❧ Though most hellebores are shameless self-seeders, you'll get alien colors. If you want something exact, divide them. All parts of the plant should take root.

❧ To divide *H. orientalis*, cut off pieces with shoots and roots attached but leave the parent undisturbed. Or remove the entire clump and cut off portions of the rhizome, making sure that each piece has root and shoots attached. Do this in early autumn and protect with a mulch for the winter.

❧ A few pests will attack these plants: greenfly needs only to be rubbed off by hand; then get rid of old flowers and stems. Slugs and snails should be removed in early spring because they'll eat a whole plant if you aren't vigilant.

Helleborus orientalis

distributed about by ants. They germinate in the autumn or winter and may take about two years to flower.

Combine hellebores with lamiums and brunnera for contrast in shapes and foliage color, spring bulbs such as *Galanthus*, snowdrops; *Eranthis*, winter aconite; narcissus and any crocus; pulmonarias; and *Arum italicum* 'Pictum'. Margery Fish liked to place this plant on banks of rivers or ponds—places where it was possible to look up at the exciting flowers.

OTHER SPECIES & CULTIVARS

H. niger, Christmas rose, has been called a fussy aristocrat, it takes forever to bloom. But the glistening white flower is worth the wait. Grows to 1 foot (30 cm); zone 3

H. foetidus: the stinking hellebore really doesn't—the scent is so faint as to be innocuous. Grows in neat 15 inch (38 cm) clumps with fan-shaped leaves. Though it is not long-lived, it self-seeds to keep the species going. It's a good cut flower. Native to Britain. Green bells in early spring. Needs really good drainage; zone 3.

H. lividus, from Majorca, like *H. corsicus* but needs a warm, sheltered garden; zone 7.

H. l. corsicus, Corsican hellebore, grows in 2 foot (60 cm) clumps with large floppy pale green flowers; toothed foliage, light green veining. Self-seeds like crazy, so don't worry if it picks up a fungus and dies off. It's a good pot plant for cold areas; zone 7.

H. purpurascens, purple hellebore, deciduous; grows to 10 inches (25 cm); zone 5.

Hosta sieboldiana

FAMILY NAME: *Liliaceae* / ZONE: 3
PHOTOGRAPHED IN: VanDusen Botanical Garden

Hosta sieboldiana

A friend of mine once groaned "All hostas look alike" when I issued an invitation to come and see my hosta berm. Nothing, of course, could be further from the truth. But some hostas are so common, so ubiquitous and used in such a dead boring manner, it's no wonder people find them dull.

Hostas can be used just about anywhere in the garden as edgers, specimens (some are humongous), fillers and in combination with dozens of other plants. They combine with almost any other woodland plant with no evident sense of competition. They will completely fill in holes left by bulbs. This huge family of 70 species has hundreds of new hybrids. It's a taxonomist's nightmare and a collector's heaven.

Each spring it's an enormous thrill to watch the new leaves poke their way shyly through the spring bulbs to open out into opaque silkiness.

What made me sit up and pay attention to this unkillable plant was the varieties of shapes in the leaves. There are huge, almost rounded ones that will pick up junk falling from trees around them, getting themselves stabbed by falling twigs; some hold moisture in their palm-shaped leaves. Others look like they have acne, they are so dimpled and pocked. Then there are the lance-shaped, firm leaves, which are the most elegant of all.

My treasures were the really tiny ones that have kept me entranced for several years. A slug could devour one of these little creatures in the matter of an hour. The early morning routine of getting them before they got the plant was quite wearing. But years later the hostas still persist in coming up in spite of these pests and the annual spring flood.

Then there are the colors. It seems impossible that there could be that many variations on green, from lime to chartreuse to deep hunter green; yellows from pale to rich gold; white, cream and yellow margins and all the glaucous, or blue-grays, that I adore.

PLANTING & MAINTENANCE TIPS

❧ This thoroughly adaptable plant will accept various light conditions from bright sun to deep shade, depending on the species. The soil can be sandy or loamy, but it must be high in organic matter and with good drainage. These are extremely hardy plants—they'll take lows of –30°F (–35°C) and, since they go into dormancy, won't succumb to the ravages of winter. In areas where there are serious freeze-thaw cycles, protect them with mulch.

❧ Slugs are the biggest pest. They start attacking as soon as the slightest showing takes place. I handpick a couple of hundred a day rather than use chemicals. See page 9 for a slug recipe.

❧ It's important to water early in the day; I've seen plants devastated by being wet and then hit by hot noonday sun; they need about 1 inch (3 cm) water a week.

❧ Add nitrogen-rich manure, leaf mold or compost as top dressing, and additional compost at least once a year.

❧ Divide in early spring or fall.

❧ This is a good plant for controlling erosion.

I have to admit, however, that I'm not the biggest fan of the flowers. Perhaps if I had a spot where I could admire them up close I might understand the niceties of these blooms. They merely look odd to me, sticking up as they do above the large leaves. I say "large" because I'm becoming enamored of the leaves on the more dwarf species, which can be viewed so that they seem all of a piece and not two different plants.

H. sieboldii is a huge family, which was known as *Funkia* when it was introduced to England in 1830. The heart-shaped glaucous leaves with deeply impressed veins are quite dramatic. *H. s.* 'Elegans' is even more bluey and puckered. And 'Frances Williams' has become justifiably one of the most popular of all the hybrids now for sale. It has large leaves with distinctive blue-gray centres, edged with pale to deep gold. This one can get enormous, so watch how you place it: it can grow to 3 feet (1 m) high and 4 feet (1.2 m) wide. The blooms, which come out in summer, are pale lavender.

I grow them with astilbes, ferns and daylilies, elbowing their way up between clumps of sweet woodruff. One of the most flexible uses I've seen was in the garden of a collector who kept a whole collection in containers, one to a pot, which she moved about, making arrangements outside her living-room window. They looked stunning. And it's easy to winter them over by simply storing them off the ground (so the pot won't get hit with frost) and out of the wind. I keep mine in the tool shed, and they seem none the worse for wear.

OTHER SPECIES & CULTIVARS

Generally speaking, the gray-blue hostas need shade, the all-green and those with yellow and white margins will take sun. The yellow ones like sun but can succumb to sun scald.

Here are just a few that I particularly like:

Some of the edgers that I use:

'Blue Moon', very blue foliage; grows 6 inches (15 cm) high.
'Ginko Craig', dwarf hybrid with blue flowers, light green lance-shaped leaves edged in white.
'Gold Drop' and 'Gold Standard', with pale lance-shaped leaves.
'Janet', foliage changes from lime green to gold to white with a touch of green; grows to 16 inches (40 cm).

H. tokudama, almost dwarf version of *H. sieboldii*, more cupped leaf, very slow growing, to 10 inches (25 cm).

H. undulata 'Albo-marginata' has white edges and may be the one that throws people off because it's everywhere.

H. ventricosa, broad glossy green leaves, violet flowers; grows to 2 feet (60 cm).
'Honeybells' has slightly wavy leaves with fragrant white flowers.

Kirengeshoma palmata

FAMILY NAME: *Saxifragaceae* / ZONE: 5
PHOTOGRAPHED IN THE GARDEN OF: Pamela Frost

I have this plant on a small rise in the shade garden, close to a shrub called *Clethra alnifolia*, which blooms at the same time. They are the glory of the August garden. All around, things are starting to slow down, but these two start their subtle dramatic performance, which goes on for weeks on end.

Russell Page admired what he called "the architectural harmony in all its parts of soft green leaves, well-articulated stalks and muted yellow hanging flowers in early autumn." He chose *Gentiana asclepiadea*, willow gentian, with its purply blue flowers, and *Tiarella cordifolia* to plant around his kirengeshomas.

In my garden I have it with *Mertensia virginica*, Virginia blue bells, which have blue flowers in April or early May, scillas by the dozen and *Erythronium*

Kirengeshoma palmata

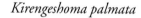

dens-canis, dogtooth violet. Nearby as good contrasts, there are *Bergenia cordifolia* and hostas. These are small grace notes because it's the foliage that matters. *Kirengeshoma palmata* foliage looks like maple leaves, though it's more open and palmate (palm-like). The stems are almost purple-green, and the higher up on the stems the less stalked the leaves become, so they look like they are part of the stem itself. The whole effect is one of quiet elegance: bright green leaves, rounded-lobed, with waxy funnel-shaped creamy yellow-green flowers. In autumn the flower buds swell up and unfold slowly in a most unspectacular way to reveal delicate ivory bells that look a bit like a campanula. The 2–inch (5 cm) flowers last for a good six weeks.

This genus is known as monotypic—that means there aren't any varieties. It grows to about 4 feet (1.2 m) with a slightly narrower spread. It stands erect, without any propping, on stems that start arching towards the top. The leaves at the top are without stalks.

This is known as a choice plant—that means it's hard to find. It looks rather unusual and many people touring the garden comment on it immediately. So put it with other choice plants such as rhodos, since they demand the same kind of culture. And the kirengeshomas bloom when the rhododendrons are out of season.

OTHER SPECIES & CULTIVARS

Kirengeshoma koreana is slightly taller and has more erect inflorescences and more open flowers.

Milium effusum 'Aureum'

FAMILY NAME: *Gramineae* / ZONE: 5 to 8
PHOTOGRAPHED IN: VanDusen Botanical Garden

Milium effusum 'Aureum' with *aubrieta*

It's hard to resist a gold plant to bring brilliance into a dark corner. Normally we think of golden plants as requiring plenty of sun. There are about six species in the family of this ornamental grass native of North America and Eurasia. The one that is most familiar is Bowles' golden grass.

Mr. Bowles was a collector and great lover of the golden plants, so whenever you see his name attached to a cultivar you know its color.

One of the delights of this plant is that you will find seedlings popping up all over like nuggets of gold scattered about. They also come true—which means they look exactly the same as the mother plant.

This tough plant will work in just about any climate. The leaves, stems and flowers are a rather attractive pastel yellow; grows to 4 feet (120 cm) in the ideal situation. The growth pattern is straight up and then arching out in a willowy manner. Though it takes a long time to establish itself (and I've had bits and pieces just disappear), it is easy to divide and spread around.

I like this plant with *Alchemilla mollis*, Lady's mantle; *Chrysanthemum parthenium* 'Aureum'; the golden form of feverfew; and with ferns; and the golden spikes next to something as strong and firm as *Polystichum acrostichoides*, Christmas fern, which is also evergreen.

Ornamental grasses are incredibly useful in almost any part of the garden, but most people forget about growing them in shade areas. A reasonable number do well in part shade, and I've listed some of them here.

Other strong additions to the shady garden are both called lilyturfs: *Ophiopogon planiscapus* 'Nigrescans', black lilyturf, and *Liriope muscari* var. *variegata*. Although grass-like, they are not grasses. Both are in the *Liliaceae* family and are great successes in shade. The liriope mentioned is a wonderful blue and yellow striped form with bright blue little pokers, and it does look like a grape hyacinth. These plants are incredibly versatile and can be used as edgers or allowed to form wide swathes (very slowly but inexorably). *Ophiopogon*, also known as Mondo Grass, is very slow to grow but is striking. Both lilyturfs grow to about 1 foot (30 cm).

Ornamental grasses come in such a variety of sizes and colors that they can be used in naturalized areas, as specimens to announce new sections of the garden and in rock gardens and containers. They add movement to a garden with lots of static plants such as evergreens, stolid shrubs or stiff trees. They shimmer in the light, move with silky ease and rustle together, adding sound to the winter garden.

PLANTING & MAINTENANCE TIPS

❧ *Milium effusum* isn't a long-lived plant, but it will keep coming back true to its own nature by seeding itself. It spreads very slowly. Out of all the ornamental grasses I have, this is the only one that my cat likes to munch on.

❧ General care of ornamental grasses: Some grasses are self-cleaning—that is, they will get rid of the winter's debris on their own. Others will need a little help by hand pulling the old stuff out. And still others like being whacked back almost to the ground so they can come back new and strong in spring.

OTHER SPECIES & CULTIVARS

Several ornamental grasses do fairly well in a semi-shaded situation. These are some of the more readily available.

Tall:

Miscanthus sinensis 'Gracillimus', Maidengrass, has a green leaf with silver in the midvein; red to pink panicles turn beige in winter; grows 4' – 6' (1.2 m – 2 m).

Molinia 'Windspiel', purple moor grass, likes a bit of moisture in the soil; blue-green leaves turn reddish brown in winter; purple panicles from July to September; grows to 6 feet (2 m);

Panicum virgatum, switch grass, can take both moist and dry conditions; has red-tinted foliage with purple panicles; leaves turn beige in winter; grows 4' – 5' (1.2 m – 1.5 m).

Spartina pectinata, 'Aureomarginata', cord grass, has shiny green leaves with yellow margins; moist, well-drained soil; grows 4' – 6' (1.2 m – 2 m).

Medium:

Andropogon scoparius, little bluestem, blue at the base of the clump, turns orangy wheat color after frost; upright foliage; grows 18" – 24" (45 cm – 60 cm) high; zone 5.

Carex pendula, sedge grass, semi-evergreen; needs moist acidic soil; pendulous blooms from June to August; grows to 30 inches (90 cm); zone 5.

Chasmanthium latifolium, northern sea oats, light green turning dark green to red-bronze in winter; humusy, well-drained soil; partial shade; grows to 3 feet (1 m).

Deschampsia caespitosa, tufted hair grass, dark green to straw in winter; delicate flowers from June until winter; grows to 2 feet (60 cm); zone 4.

Helictotrichon sempervirens, blue oat grass, steely blue turning to wheat flowers; tolerates poor soil, needs good drainage; grows to 3 feet (1 m); zone 4. A stunner.

Hystrex patula, bottle brush grass, light green inflorescence; grows to 4 feet (1.2 m); native to shady woodlands; zone 5.

Phalaris arundinacea var. *picta*, gardener's garters, white or pink inflorescence June to July. Incredibly invasive, so it's important to keep it from spreading everywhere. Shear off the tops regularly to restrain its movement. Grows to 2 feet (60 cm); zone 4.

Short:

Arrhenatherum elatius var. *bulbosum* 'Variegatum', open, erect plant with white and bluey green striped leaves; grows to 12 inches (30 cm); a real beauty that doesn't spread quickly; can be shabby in hot summer and must be cut back once; zone 4.

Carex morrowii 'Variegata', variegated sedge grass, grows to 18 inches (45 cm); yellow, green and white striped leaves, silver flowers; grows to 12 inches (30 cm); zone 5.

Festuca glauca, blue fescue, blue-green very fine leaves, semi-evergreen; grows to 12 inches (30 cm); zone 5.

Hakonechloa macra 'Aureola', bright yellow, looks like it's constantly windswept; a grand plant for containers. Very slow grower; grows to 18 inches (45 cm); zone 4.

Molinia caerulea 'Variegata', variegated moor grass, yellow and green striped leaves; yellow, green or purple flowers in June; grows to 2 feet (60 cm); zone 4.

Omphalodes cappadocica

FAMILY NAME: *Boraginaceae* / ZONE: 6; 5 to 9 depending on species
PHOTOGRAPHED IN THE GARDEN OF: Helen and Don Nesbitt

The early spring garden is a glory with bulbs blooming everywhere. And then there's the day when, in concert, they all droop and start to turn ugly colors. Combining bulbs with perennials is a must. *Omphalodes* is one of the best.

Omphalodes cappadocica, from Asia, grows in thick clumps of almost heart-shaped leaves and incredibly blue flowers that grow on upright stems. As a ground cover it tends not to be invasive. This is a good plant for zone 6 and warmer. The gray-green basal leaves are 4" – 5" (10 cm –

Omphalodes cappadocica

12.5 cm) long and the flowers float above them. A sweep of them is breath-taking.

The warmer the area, the more likely it will stay evergreen throughout the winter. 'Anthea Bloom' is paler, with more of a gray tinge to the foliage. The clumps reach about 12 inches (30 cm) and the flowers come out in succession over a number of weeks from spring into early summer. It travels by creeping rhizomes.

There are 24 species of this plant, and they make a pleasant carpet of color. Because it spreads quickly and has a fairly benign root system, plant it with spring bulbs such as crocus and erythronium. I use it to dwarf narcissus such as 'Tête à tête' and 'Jack Snipe' because their foliage takes so long to disappear it can make the hapless gardener impatient (yet it's important to leave that foliage alone to make the bulb's food for the following spring).

It can be difficult to establish ground covers under trees, and I've found the best is *Lysimachia nummularia*, creeping Jenny, because it's easy to remove once other plants have established themselves. Meanwhile it will hold back weeds. *Thymus serpyllum*, mother of thyme; golden oregano; and *Mentha requienii*, Corsican mint, are all good shade ground covers. For other ground cover suggestions, see page 8.

OTHER SPECIES & CULTIVARS

O. verna, blue-eyed Mary, creeping forget-me-not. Trailing plants that spread by underground stolons. The fine-textured leaves around the base are rounded and about 4 inches (10 cm) across. In milder zones it will stay evergreen all winter. The brilliant blue flowers are larger than forget-me-nots. This is a lower creeping plant about 8 inches (20 cm) high with the same dark green heart-shaped leaves. Good ground cover under trees and can take very deep shade.

'Alba', white flowers, spreads by stolons; the bloom is short but worth it. Grows 4 inches (10 cm) high with a 2 foot (60 cm) spread; zone 6.

O. luciliae, rock garden plant, blue-gray leaves, sky blue flowers; likes full sun; grows 6 inches (15 cm) high with an 18 inch (45 cm) spread; zone 6.

Polygonatum multiflorum

FAMILY NAME: *Liliaceae* / ZONE: 4
PHOTOGRAPHED IN THE GARDEN OF: Kathy Leishman

Polygonatum multiflorum

The curious name of Solomon's–seal comes from the signet-shaped rootstock scars. There are more than 60 species and a large group of hybrids. *Polygonatum multiflorum*, Eurasian Solomon's–seal, and *P. odoratum* are native to Europe and Asia. The former has cylindrical stems that grow to a comfortable 2' – 4' (60 cm – 1.2 m), with leaves that are 2" – 6" (10 cm – 15 cm) long. *P. biflorum*, eastern North American, has yellowish white tubular flowers with bell-shaped corollas in May. *P. biflorum* and *P. commutatum* are large plants with hairless stems and once established can cope in woodland conditions that are occasionally dry.

These are wonderful plants for shady borders in the woodland or as a naturalized planting. The plant spreads by rhizomes that inch along almost horizontally through the soil. The stalks stand straight up without any branches and are adorned with alternate lance-shaped leaves that create green layers (or green and white in the variegated version). The farther up the stalk the leaves grow, the more the plant tips over into a graceful arch. The flowers, hanging in clusters of four to seven, are usually white, ecru, greenish or occasionally a little pink.

Under the right woodland conditions, they grow about a foot (30 cm) a year. In my less-than-ideal woodland under greedy shallow-rooted trees, they barely creep at all, perhaps a few inches a year, which is fine with me. Too large a clump and they'd have to be confined. If they ever did make a great burst, I'd be tempted to take a chunk and put it in a container for a shady part of the deck. This is definitely the kind of plant to have in a spot where you can easily look into the face of the splendid flowers.

I've never tried forcing *Polygonatum* but pass on the following as an intriguing recommendation: plant divisions in pots during the fall. They can either be left in a cold protected place or put into a plunge bed—a spot where pots are buried almost to the rim in sand or peat moss. When you want to start forcing them, lift them out and bring indoors to a cool spot. Once temperatures reach 55°F (12°C), they will start growing. After blooming, put them back into the garden. This can't be done year after year with the same plant.

Surrounded by shorter plants, they look as though they are rising out of them with great dignity: hostas, ferns, astilbes, aquilegias and gentians are mates to match this elegant plant. And, of course, they should have lots of

PLANTING & MAINTENANCE TIPS

❧ This is an easy plant to grow in moist soil, and nearly full shade; it will tolerate sun in northern areas, but must have shade from morning sun in the south. Once they are firmly established, most species tolerate dry conditions under trees—even evergreens—with the exception of *P. commutatum*. You'll know when they are too crowded—the flowers stop being profuse. Dig them up and divide in early spring or early fall. Plant about 2 feet (60 cm) apart and keep mulched with leaf mold and compost.

Polygonatum multiflorum

small spring bulbs such as scilla and grape hyacinth planted alongside as well. One of my favorite moments is when *Narcissus* var. *triandrus* 'Thalia', flowers. This narcissus has three blooms at the top of the stem and is the same height as the Solomon's–seal nearby. As the latter continues to grow, the narcissus slowly fades into oblivion.

OTHER SPECIES & CULTIVARS

P. biflorum, leaves have pale downy undersides; greenish white flowers hang in pairs. This North American native prefers acid soil. Makes dense clumps fairly quickly; mulch with pine needles; grows to 1' – 3' (30 cm – 1 m).

P. commutatum, great or giant Solomon's–seal; this North American native is twice the size of European species, and at 7 feet (2 m) is the largest form there is. The oblong green leaves grow to 10 inches (25 cm), and the clusters of bell-shaped white flowers emerge in late spring to bloom in June for about two weeks. It has black berries in September. This is a handsome plant with tall, arching stems.

P. odoratum 'Variegatum', pairs of fragrant greenish white flowers in early spring followed by black berries; stems to 1½ feet (45 cm); oval to lance-shaped green leaves. The variegation is rather subtle from pink to glaucous to cream. Once it's established, this species can be divided as often as you wish.

Primula japonica

FAMILY NAME: *Primulaceae* / ZONE: 5; from 2 depending on the species
PHOTOGRAPHED IN THE GARDENS OF: Lyn Noble and VanDusen Botanical Garden

Primroses come in just about every color imaginable. They need little attention, and there are native species that can be grown almost everywhere on the continent, including Alaska.

There are at least 500 members of this genus, and they've been subdivided into 30 sections, most coming from the Northern Hemisphere. No matter what conditions you garden in, there will be a primula that's just

Primula japonica

right for you, from windy cliffs to boggy low spots. They thrive in shade or indirect light. And if they must have sun—a half day is enough—the alpines and subtropicals prefer full morning or afternoon sun. Meadow and woodland species prefer filtered shade.

Primula japonica, the candelabra primrose, is one of the hardiest species and comes in a wide range of colors from white to crimson, copper, red, salmon, apricot and violet with dark or yellow eyes. This self-seeder will form a large colony if the conditions are right. Their flowering season in some areas is from May to July. They do need protection against the sun, so plant them in areas of dappled or half shade—indirect light—in moist conditions. It has layers of flowers in whorls around the stem. As the stem grows, more flowers are produced. These florets are 1 inch (2.5 cm) and the stems can grow 1' – 2' (30 cm – 60 cm). The leaves are slightly wrinkled with toothed edges in pale green. The bold upright plants form into clumps. These are among the easiest to grow if you are a first-time primula fancier. Zone 5.

PLANTING & MAINTENANCE TIPS

❧ Needs moist soil with excellent drainage. Add lots of organic matter and mulch in winter, especially in northern areas. They can be divided every three years or when they get crowded. Do this immediately after flowering.

❧ The colder the climate, the thicker a blanket of mulch you will need to put over a bed of primula. They should have protection from winter winds no matter where you live.

❧ Pests that love this plant: slugs, which can be handpicked, and red spider mites, which can be washed off with a hit of water from the hose.

❧ Sow seeds in fall and make sure they are covered by snow or are well mulched so they will remain moist. Uncover first thing in spring. Or put plants in during the fall.

❧ Sow seed outdoors in flats or cold frames early in spring in a mix of compost and sandy loam. Use very shallow plantings, cover with sand or vermiculite and make sure it doesn't dry out (a plastic cover or glass will help, but make sure the ventilation is good).

❧ You can plant a potted primrose outside in spring. It will rebloom the following year.

Primula japonica

OTHER SPECIES & CULTIVARS

Auricula primulas:

P. auricula: this is a whole category of *Primula*. They have smooth, fleshy 4–inch (10 cm) long leaves; grows 6" – 8" (15 cm – 20 cm) high; May blooms come in a wide range of colors from yellow and pink to mauve, blue, cream and orange. They have shallow roots and should be mulched; zone 3.

Candelabra primulas:

P. denticulata, Himalayan primrose, has long-lasting, globe-like pink, purple, red or white blooms that stick up over other spring flowers. Bright shade is preferable to direct sun. Must have good drainage and doesn't like wet winter conditions. Grows to 1 foot (30 cm); zone 4.

'Alba' is a gorgeous white form with 2–inch (5 cm) scented flowers.

P. x *polyantha*, polyanthus, cowslip. An old-fashioned flower of the first order, fragrant, informal, with varieties of many colors and types, blooms in May; zone 3.

Vernalis primulas:

P. veris, cowslip, is the most adaptable, probably the easiest to grow; zone 5.

P. elatior, oxlip primrose, has yellow flowers; zone 5.

P. vulgaris, meadow primrose, the real English primrose, yellow, purple or blue flowers on short stems; zone 3.

Asian primroses:

P. sieboldii and *P. kisoana* are Asian primroses and usually have delicate flowers and hairy leaves. They can withstand more sun than other species, hate winter wet, and good drainage is essential; zone 4.

Thalictrum delavayi

'Hewitt's Double'

FAMILY NAME: *Ranunculaceae* / ZONE: 5
PHOTOGRAPHED IN THE GARDEN OF: Valerie Pfeiffer

This glorious plant would make a strong statement in any border, but its stately demeanor is especially important in a shady one. The lacy effect of the deeply cut leaves works well with small plants or ones of equal architectural value. The delicate flowers have an airy sparkle to them.

On a north-facing border with only a few hours of afternoon sun, I have a *Thalictrum rochebrunianum* near a group of late-blooming lilies, a *Cimicifuga simplex* and low-growing hardy geraniums. I don't think it's important to always have large plants at the rear of borders. In fact, that can get to be an incredible bore. I started with a meadow rue and worked to have other plants about the same height, as a punctuation mark, or a stopping point for the eye at the front of a long border. What lies past them becomes a bit of a mystery—the visitor has to get into the garden to find out what's beyond this delicate wall of foliage.

The *Ranunculaceae* family, which also contains buttercups and clematises,

PLANTING & MAINTENANCE TIPS

❧ This is a pretty easy plant to look after. The only caution is not to work too closely to the plant in early spring, since they come out of dormancy fairly late and you don't want to be stomping on their territory. It's also wise not to let the plant get dried out. Meadow rues like dappled or part shade. Any soil will do if lightened up with lots of moisture-retentive organic matter. Overfertilizing leads to weak growth. Some of the larger varieties might have to be staked, though I tend to chop them back severely after flowering so that a new flush of leaves will come along.

❧ Divide in spring just before new growth starts showing—it may look a bit grumpy for a while. It's an easy plant to start from seed indoors or directly outside in May.

Thalictrum aquilegifolium

is huge. In the genus we're dealing with here, there are 150 species, natives of the Northern Hemisphere. They are all deciduous and many are alpine or boreal, prized in the rock garden.

The scientific naming of plants is always under constant review and revision. It takes time and money to change labels and signs to confirm the recent nomenclature changes. *T. delavayi* 'Hewitt's Double' is a case in point. In the trade it is often sold as *T. dipterocarpum* 'Hewitt's Double'. It's all very bewildering. What you are looking for is a plant with a double lilac flower, prominent yellow stamens and divided green leaves. Blooms in mid- to late summer, and the flowers last for weeks. Grows to 3 feet (1 m). Can be increased only by division.

'Album' has white flowers.

The ease with which thalictrums fit into a garden is surpassed only by the ease of looking after them. The flowers are not big show stoppers, but they are almost without blemish or pest. The foliage in most cases has a glaucous or blue cast.

Use as part of the edge of a woodland garden, with Siberian iris; columbines; goatsbeard; and hardy geraniums.

OTHER SPECIES & CULTIVARS

T. adiantifolium has foliage like the maidenhair fern. Grows to 1½ feet (45 cm).

T. aquilegifolium, columbine meadow-rue, is a native of Europe and North America. Gray-green foliage; lilac to purple-pink flowers in May and June. Will take sun to partial shade; tolerates some drought. Has hollow stems, divided leaflets, erect flowers in many-branched panicles. Grows 2' – 3' (60 cm – 1 m) high. This is the easiest of the thalictrums to grow. The foliage is indeed like columbine, thus the name.

'Album' has white flowers.

'Thundercloud' is a glorious form with steely blue foliage and purple flowers.

T. flavum has blue-green very divided foliage with creamy yellow flowers; the show is in the stamens; sepals drop quickly. Blooms June to August. Grows 4' – 5' (1.2 m – 1.5 m) high and spreads into clumps. It's the least interesting of the ones I have.

T. kiusianum, a small plant that makes a good pot plant or background for bonsai; grows to 4 inches (10 cm); native of Japan.

T. rochebrunianum is a plant I let go to seed because it looks so absolutely gorgeous in the garden when the purple flower heads have dried on their long stems.

T. speciosissimum (syn. *T. glaucum*) has gorgeous blue-gray foliage with soft yellow flowers; grows to 5 feet (1.5 m). I have it next to one of my favorite plants, *Alchemilla mollis.*

Tiarella trifoliata

FAMILY NAME: *Saxifragaceae* / ZONE: 3
PHOTOGRAPHED IN THE GARDEN OF: Karen Morgan

Here is a plant that can honestly be described as charming. It grows in clumps with long, stalked leaves; some species are evergeen, others deciduous. The white flowers that rise in soft pokers above the basal leaves provide the enchantment. The common name, foamflower, is accurate. A drift of these small plants in spring is like a soft white cloud of smoke rising gently above soft green leaves.

There are six species in the genus, which is part of a huge family, Saxifragaceae, and they are generally native to North America. This makes

Tiarella trifoliata

them tough plants, hardy to almost any region in shady borders and wood-land gardens. Depending on the species, they will bloom sometime between April and July for up to six weeks in the right conditions. As a ground cover under trees and as erosion control on a hillside, you couldn't ask for anything lovelier, especially in autumn when the foliage in most species turns a brilliant color.

The plants grow by either rhizomes or stolons that won't inhibit the growth of larger plants that grow through and around them. The compact size, 12" – 18" (30 cm – 45 cm), makes them an excellent ground cover. The foliage is mostly basal and is very sensuous. The flowers clustering at the end of the stems have five green sepals, the same number of petals and 10 long stamens. This wonderful symmetry is something to be alert to in the garden.

T. trifoliata has 8–inch (20 cm) stems and palmate leaves with three lobes 4 inches (10 cm) wide; native to the Pacific Northwest.

These plants look exquisite as background and complement the early spring bulbs.

PLANTING & MAINTENANCE TIPS

❧ Prefers moist, humus-rich, slightly acidic soil. Divide clumps every two or three years. Propagate by root division in spring or fall. These plants take a fair amount of shade but grow fastest in partial shade.

OTHER SPECIES & CULTIVARS

T. cordifolia has clusters of broad, round to heart-shaped leaves, 5 inches (12 cm) wide, that rise from long slim stolons; they might be a bit rampant for some small gardens, since they grow rather aggressively in tufts. The soft leaves have three to five lobes and are rounded with toothed edges; airy spikes of white, sometimes pink or red flowers with oblong petals bloom from April to July. Native to Eastern North America.

T. c. 'Purpurea' has even more arresting foliage in bronzy purple.

T. unifoliata, a rugged West Coast native that grows from Alaska to California. This is the only one of the tiarellas that can tolerate any sort of drought. Dark leaves with white flowers.

T. wherryi is an eastern native related to *T. cordifolia* but lacking stolons. It also has a more flashy bloom in a salmon pink or white over tufts of deep green leaves. To keep it looking fresh, divide regularly—as often as every two years. It is very slow to establish itself, but is considered the choicest of the lot.

Trillium erectum
forma *albiflorum*

FAMILY NAME: *Liliaceae* / ZONE: 3
PHOTOGRAPHED IN: VanDusen Botanical Garden

Trillium erectum forma *albiflorum*

The very first trillium that came into my garden was a gift from a neighbor's garden. It took the two of us and a couple of garden spades with sharp edges to wrest part of the plant away from her garden. I now understand the great will to survive of this fragile-looking plant.

It is rumored that it is on the endangered species list. Yes and no. In some parts of the country, the plants you see in nurseries have been collected in the wild. If we keep taking them from the wild, many species will indeed be at risk. However, take them from places that are about to be damaged or bulldozed. Better for them to be safe in your garden than obliterated.

⁂ Trilliums are not fussy plants. Although they increase slowly, they are very long-lived. The most active root growth is in early fall. Planting and transplanting should be done mid-September. Set tubers fairly deep, covered by about 4 inches (10 cm) of soil, then add a mulch of compost or leaf mold.

⁂ Division is the easiest way to expand your stock. Wait until the flowers have gone but before the plant disappears for the summer.

These plants flower before trees begin to leaf out, making them a great treasure for the spring garden. There are 20 species of trilliums in two types: pedunculate—the flowers are above the leaves; or sessile, with no stalks so the flowers appear to sit on the leaf.

The roots are tuber-like rhizomes growing straight down, hanging on for dear life from the main tuber. The more than 30 native North American species have the familiar three leaves—single stem with single flower at the top; flowers also come in clusters of three petals, three green sepals.

Trillium erectum, wake-robin or stinking Benjamin, is pedunculate. Like hellebores, this one forms clumps up to 1 foot (30 cm) tall. It tolerates more shade than some other trilliums. Its wine red flowers bloom in May, followed by dark red berries. Native to central and eastern North America. *T. e. albiflorum* is a western species not recommended for eastern gardens.

Combine trilliums with other native plants such as *Phlox divaricata*, hardy blue phlox; *Adiantum pedatum*, maidenhair fern; or any of the shade-loving hardy geraniums; and with epimediums, violas and the small spikes of *Milium effusum* 'Aureum', Bowles' golden grass. They are naturals with almost any hosta and pulmonarias (lungworts), which will graciously take over when they disappear.

OTHER SPECIES & CULTIVARS

T. grandiflorum, white trillium, native to eastern North America, is the showiest and the easiest to grow. Shiny bronze new growth and yellow buds eventually develop into rounded green leaves to 6 inches (15 cm) with white flowers that fade to pink with age. Neutral soil and protection from sun are important. Grows wild from Quebec to the American Midwest. This plant varies a great deal, and in some places it has close to pink petals, sometimes almost green. Grows 9" – 18" (23 cm – 45 cm).

T. nivale, white or snow trillium, is like a miniature *T. grandiflorum*, 3" – 6" (7.5 cm – 15 cm) high with wide elliptic leaves. Native to eastern United States; zone 6.

T. ovatum, native from British Columbia to central California, portent of spring, with smaller stalked flowers and narrower petals than its eastern relative.

Viola labradorica

FAMILY NAME: *Violaceae* / ZONE: 3
PHOTOGRAPHED IN THE GARDEN OF: Kathy Leishman

When this plant was first given to me I was promised that it would spread like mad. Not in my garden, it didn't. Maybe the shade is too dense for fast coverage. I don't care, because this delightful plant shows up in odd little places—always a surprise and usually better than I could place it.

Pansies and violets are often confused, so it's worthwhile to make a distinction here. There are 500 species in the Violaceae family, which includes pansies, the hybrids we know and grow as annuals, and violas, the perennials

Viola labradorica

under discussion here. Violas, or violets, are smaller-flowered than pansies and are often sold under species names.

Violas are perennial forms of pansies derived from the wildflower *Viola cornuta*. The whole family is native to northern temperate zones and the Andes. All violets have flowers that are similar: the lower petal is spurred, and the four pairs of upper petals have a different size and color. They start blooming in late spring and some of the native species continue to bloom all summer.

The viola we're most familiar with is *Viola tricolor* var. *hortensis*, Johnny-jump-up. It's been used as a medicinal herb for centuries but didn't come into cultivation until the sixteenth century. And serious work with it didn't begin until the nineteenth century. *V. odorata*, sweet violet of gardens, *V. canina* and *V. tricolor* have been used since ancient times as medicinal herbs.

Viola labradorica purpurea is very special. The dark purple-green leaves have a tiny dancing dark purple flower that grows 2 inches (5 cm) with a spread of 8 inches (20 cm). It's so unobtrusive that it is easy to overlook, but the startling dense purple foliage makes it a favorite ground cover.

Given the deep foliage color, these violas look wonderful next to anything—hostas, for instance. I have tiny hostas and violas as edgers in one shady border. The effect is of delicacy and lightness. I have one viola that

PLANTING & MAINTENANCE TIPS

❧ In milder regions violas bloom all winter. No matter where these plants are grown, they all like cool, moisture-retentive soil. If it becomes very hot, they may die off after blooming but before producing seed. If this happens, treat them like annuals and plant them each spring. The warmer the area, the more important it is to keep them out of the morning sun and provide lots of water. Add compost and manure at least once a year.

❧ Divide up in spring or fall. Pinch out the runners in spring to make stronger plants.

❧ Plant with the crown at the same level as the soil.

❧ Violas make super container plants. Keep them in a cool place under a high canopy. Keep them deadheaded.

❧ Seeds can be started indoors 10 to 12 weeks before the last frost for flowering by late spring. They will often resow in the garden, especially in cooler regions.

self-seeds about the garden and comes up in different forms from one year to another. It doesn't matter whether it is blue one year or purple the next, it always looks good.

Violas are delicious to eat. A few added to a salad not only look pretty, they add a certain piquancy to the flavor.

OTHER SPECIES & CULTIVARS

V. canadensis has heart-shaped leaves; white-tinged purple flowers with a yellow eye—the lower petals have purple veins; native to North America; grows 12 inches (30 cm) with the same spread; zone 3.

V. cornuta, horned violet, tufted pansy, is a native of the Pyrenees. It will make a carpet of green. The tall stems have lilac-blue flowers in summer. Deadhead or shear to encourage flowering. Grows 6" – 12" (15 cm – 30 cm) high, with a spread of 12" – 15" (30 cm – 38 cm); zone 5.

'Purpurea' has purple petals.

V. c. 'White Perfection' has perfect white flowers; good edger.

V. odorata, sweet violet, is a European and Asian native that lives up to its name in the delicious scent of both foliage and flowers. It comes in a wide range of violet hues. Blooms in spring and fall; heart-shaped leaves. In mild climates, it flowers from March and perhaps even earlier. It is equally at home in the sun and the shade. Good spreader. Grows 6" – 12" (15 cm – 30 cm) high. There are dozens of wonderful cultivars in a wide range of colors from pink to blue to pure white. Here are a few: 'Royal Robe' (purple); 'Queen Charlotte' (blue); 'Red Giant' (red); 'White Czar' (white).

V. tricolor, Johnny-jump-up, has the familiar two-colored yellow and purple flowers with dark lines. They spread by seed and will grow up to 12 inches (30 cm) in part shade.

'Jolly Joker' is a larger version with deep purple and orange flowers.

V. riviniana, wood violet; short erect rhizome; European native with round dark purple leaves that turn green by the end of the season; blue-violet petals. Self-seeding; zone 3.

Bibliography

The American Horticultural Society Encyclopedia of Garden Plants. New York: Macmillan, 1989.

Ashley, Anne & Peter. *The Canadian Plant Sourcebook.* Ottawa: 1990.

Druse, Ken. *The Natural Shade Garden.* New York: Clarkson Potter, 1992.

Fish, Margery. *Gardening in the Shade.* London: Faber and Faber, 1983.

Harris, Marjorie. *The Canadian Gardener's Guide to Foliage & Garden Design.* Toronto: Random House, 1993.

Hortus Third. New York: Macmillan, 1976.

McGourty, Frederick. *The Perennial Gardener.* Boston: Houghton Mifflin, 1989.

Paterson, Allen. *Plants for Shade and Woodland.* Markham: Fitzhenry & Whiteside, 1987.

Sabuco, John J. *The Best of the Hardiest.* 3rd ed. Flossmoor, Ill.: Plantsmen's Publications, 1990.

Schenk, George. *The Complete Shade Gardener.* Boston: Houghton Mifflin, 1984.

Magazines:
Canadian Gardening; Fine Gardening; Gardens West; Horticulture; The Island Gardener; National Gardening; Plant & Garden.

ZONE CHART		
Zone 1	below −50°F	(below −45°C)
Zone 2	−50 to −40°F	(−45 to −40°C)
Zone 3	−40 to −30°F	(−40 to −35°C)
Zone 4	−30 to −20°F	(−35 to −30°C)
Zone 5	−20 to −10°F	(−30 to −23°C)
Zone 6	−10 to 0°F	(−23 to −18°C)
Zone 7	0 to 10°F	(−18 to −12°C)
Zone 8	10 to 20°F	(−12 to −7°C)
Zone 9	20 to 30°F	(−7 to −1°C)
Zone 10	30 to 40°F	(−1 to 4°C)

Index

A

acid leaf mold, 7
Aconitum x *bicolor*, 11
  A. carmichaelii, 11; *A. henryi*, 10-11;
  A. h. 'Sparks Variety', 11; *A. napellus*,
  10-11, 11; *A. n.* 'Bressingham Spire',
  11; *A. septentrionale* 'Ivorine', 11
Actaea pachypoda, 13
Adiantum pedatum, 12-13, 58
Ajuga pyramidalis, 8
  A. reptans 'Burgundy Glow', 8
Alchemilla mollis, 6, 14-15, 42, 54
  A. x *splendens*, 15; *A. vulgaris* see *A. mollis*
Andropogon scoparius, 43
Anemone japonica, 17, 23
Arrhenatherum elatius var. *bulbosum*
  'Variegatum', 43
Arum italicum 'Pictum', 35;
Asarum canadense, 8
  A. caudatum, 8; *A. europaeum*, 8
Asian primrose, 51
Asplenium platyneuron, 13
Astilbe x *arendsii*:
  'Bridal Veil', 16, 17; 'Cattleya', 18;
  'Ostrich Plume', 18; 'Sparton', 18;
  A. chinensis 'Pumila', 18; *A.* var. *davidii*, 18;
  A. simplicifolia 'Sprite', 17, 18;
  A. taquetii, 18; *A. t.* 'Superba', 18
Athyrium filix-femina, 13
  A. goeringianum 'Pictum', 13
Aubrieta, 41, 43
auricula primulas, 51

B

balloon, 20
baneberry, 13
barrenwort, 9, 26-7
bellflower, 19
Berberidaceae family, 26
bergenia, heartleaf, 8
Bergenia cordifolia, 8, 40
  B. crassifolia, 8
berm, 4
bishop's hat, 26-7
bleeding heart, 24-5
bloodroot, 13, 33
blue bells, Virginia, 39
blue-eyed Mary, 8, 44-5
bluebells-of-Scotland, 21
blueberry, 9
Boittonia asteriodes, 23
Boraginaceae family, 44-5
Bowles' golden grass, 41-3, 58
bugbane, 22-3
bugle flower, 8
bunchberry, 8

C

Campanula alliariifolia, 20, 21
  C. carpatica, 21; 'Blue Clips', 21; 'White
  Clips', 20, 21; *C. cochleariifolia*, 21;
  C. glomerata, 21; *C. lactiflora*, 19, 20;
  'Alba', 20; 'Loddon Anna', 20;
  C. latifolia, 21; 'Alba', 21; 'Macrantha',
  21; *C. persicifolia*, 20, 21; 'Alba', 21;
  'Telham Beauty', 21; *C.*
  portenschlagiana, 5, 21; *C. poscharskyana*,
  21; *C. apunculoides*, 20; *C. rotundifolia*,
  21; *C. r.* var. *alba*, 21
Campanulaceae family, 19
candelabra primulas, 51
Carex morrowii 'Variegata', 43
  C. pendula, 43
Caulophyllum thalictroides, 13
Chasmanthium latifolium, 43
Christmas:
  fern, 42; rose, 33-5
Chrysanthemum parthenium 'Aureum', 42
Cimicifuga, 17
  C. ramosa, 22, 23; *C. r.* var. *cordifolia*,
  23; *C. simplex*, 52; 'White Pearl', 23;
  C. s. ramosa 'Atropurpurea', 22-3;
  'Brunette', 23
clay soil, 7
Clethra alnifolia, 39
cohosh, 13, 22-3
columbine meadow-rue, 54
composting, 7
Cornus alba 'Sibirica', 29
  C. canadensis, 8
Corydalis lutea, 25
Cotoneaster dielsianus, 23
country gardens, 16
cowslip, 51
cranberry, 9
cranesbill, 30-2
  Armenian, 32
creeping Jenny, 8, 14
crocus, 35
Cypripedium acaule, 13

D

dappled shade, 6
daylily, 23
deadnettle, 8
dense shade, 6
Deschampsia caespitosa, 43
Dicentra cucullaria, 25
  D. eximia, 24, 25; *D. formosa*, 25; 'Adrian
  Bloom', 25; 'Alba', 25; 'Luxuriant', 24-5;
  D. spectabilis, 25; 'Alba', 25
dogtooth violet, 28-9, 39-40
dried flowers, 16
Dryopteris filix-mas, 13
  'Cristata', 13
Dutchman's-breeches, 25

E

environment, and shade plants, 5
Epimedium grandiflorum, 27
  'Violaceum', 27; *E.* x *rubrum*, 27;
  E. x *versicolor* 'Sulphureum', 27;
  E. x *youngianum*, 26-7; 'Niveum', 27;
  'Rose Queen', 27
Eranthis, 35
erosion control, 37
Erythronium californicum, 29
  'Pagoda', 29; 'White Beauty', 29;
  E. dens-canis, 28-9, 39-40; 'Lilac

Wonder', 29; 'White Splendor', 29;
  E. oregonum, 28, 29; *E. tuolumnense*, 28-9

F

fawn lily, 28-9
fern(s), 12-13, 23
  care of, 13; Christmas, 13; cinnamon,
  13; crested male, 13; interrupted, 13;
  lady, 13; ostrich, 13; Royal, 13
Festuca glauca, 43
fiddleheads, 13
Fish, Margery, 10, 35
foamflower, 8-9, 55-6
forget-me-not, 45
freeze-thaw cycle, 7-8
Fumariaceae family, 24
Funkia, 38

G

Galanthus, 35
Galax aphylla, 8
  G. urceolata see *G. aphylla*
Galium odoratum, 8
garden design, for shade, 8
Gaultheria procumbens, 8
Gentiana asclepiadea, 39
Geraniaceae family, 30
Geranium:
  x 'Johnson's Blue', 30-2; *G. endressii*, 32;
  'Wargrave Pink', 32; *G. macrorrhizum*,
  32; 'Ingwersen's Variety', 32;
  G. m. album, 32; *G. maculatum*, 31;
  G. pratense, 32; *G. psilostetemon*, 32
ginger:
  European, 8; wild, 8
Gramineae family, 41
grasses, ornamental, 43
ground covers, 8-9, 14-15, 45

H

Hakonechloa macra 'Aureola', 43
half shade, 6
hardpan, 7
Helichrysum petiolatum, 14
Helictotrichon sempervirens, 43
hellebore, 17
Helleborus argutifolius, 33-5
  H. foetidus, 35; *H. lividus*, 34, 35;
  H. l. corsicus, 35; *H. niger*, 33-4, 35;
  H. orientalis, 34, 35; *H. purpurascens*, 35
Heuchera sanguinea 'Palace Purple', 15
Hosta sieboldiana:
  'Blue Moon', 38; 'Frances Williams',
  36-8; 'Ginko Craig', 38; 'Gold Drop',
  38; 'Gold Standard', 38; 'Janet', 38;
  H. tokudama, 38; *H. undulata* 'Albo-
  marginata', 38; *H. ventricosa*, 38;
  'Honeybells', 38
Hydrangea petiolaris, 8
Hystrex patula, 43

I

indicator plants, 4

J

Johnny-jump-up, 60, 61